FUN FACT FILE: WOMEN IN HISTORY

20 FUN FACTS ABOUT WOMEN IN COLONIAL AMERICA

By Amy Hayes

Gareth Stevens
PUBLISHING

Please visit our website, www.garethstevens.com. For a free color catalog of all our high-quality books, call toll free 1-800-542-2595 or fax 1-877-542-2596.

Cataloging-in-Publication Data

Hayes, Amy.
20 fun facts about women in colonial America / by Amy Hayes.
p. cm. — (Fun fact file: women in history)
Includes index.
ISBN 978-1-4824-2820-9 (pbk.)
ISBN 978-1-4824-2821-6 (6 pack)
ISBN 978-1-4824-2822-3 (library binding)
1. Women — United States — History — 17th century — Juvenile literature. 2. Women — United States — History — 18th century — Juvenile literature. 3. United States — Social life and customs — To 1775 — Juvenile literature. I. Hayes, Amy. II. Title.
HQ1416 H39 2016
305.4'0973'09032—d23

First Edition

Published in 2016 by
Gareth Stevens Publishing
111 East 14th Street, Suite 349
New York, NY 10003

Designer: Samantha DeMartin
Editor: Kristen Rajczak

Photo credits: Cover, p. 1 SuperStock/SuperStock/Getty Images; p. 5 Education Images/Universal Images Group Editorial/Getty Images; pp. 6, 8, 14 MPI/Archive Photos/Getty Images; p. 7 David Jackson/Wikimedia Commons; pp. 9, 24 Kean Collection/Archive Photos/Getty Images; p. 10 Ealdgyth/Wikimedia Commons; p. 11 Berents/Shutterstock.com; p. 12 Frederic Lewis/Archive Photos/Getty Images; pp. 13, 18, 20 Hulton Archive/Hulton Archive/Getty Images; p. 15 Heritage Images/Hulton Archive/Getty Images; p. 16 UniversalImagesGroup/Universal Images Group Editorial/Getty Images; p. 17 Jeff Greenberg/Photolibrary/Getty Images; p. 19 New England Chromo. Lith. Co./Wikimedia Commons; p. 21 courtesy of the Library of Congress; p. 22 Lumos3/Wikimedia Commons; p. 23 (headline) Alexander Purdie/Wikimedia Commons; p. 23 (front page) William Parks/Wikimedia Commons; p. 25 Rischgitz/Hulton Archive/Getty Images; p. 26 Louis S. Glanzman/National Geographic/Getty Images; p. 29 Harvey Barrison/Wikimedia Commons.

Printed in the United States of America

CPSIA compliance information: Batch #CS15GS: For further information contact Gareth Stevens, New York, New York at 1-800-542-2595.

Contents

Words in the glossary appear in **bold** type the first time they are used in the text.

Women of Colonial America

Women living during **colonial** times had a lot to overcome. They had to create a life for themselves in a New World! Native American women had to learn to live with new neighbors, while European and African women had to set up their lives in a place that was completely new to them.

Many colonial women were taught they weren't equal to men, and their rights were few. Yet, without women's hard work, life in the New World would have been impossible!

The colonial period in North America lasted from the founding of the first European colonies in the 1500s to the end of the American Revolution in 1783. During this time, women's jobs were mostly **domestic**.

5

FACT 1

Colonial women ran their households.

While men were considered the head of the household in the eyes of the law, it was the women of the house who made sure everything got done. Women were in charge of cooking and cleaning.

A colonial woman's most important job was caring for her children.

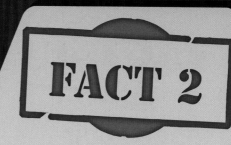

Many colonial women didn't eat with forks or knives.

Most colonial families couldn't afford metal utensils, or the tools used for eating. To eat, families used **trenchers** and spoons. Most colonial women only had one pot to make dinner. More pots meant more cleanup!

trencher

Women made their own soap!

Making soap was a long, hard job including many hours spent over the fire. Some common **ingredients** used to make soap were animal fat, ashes from the family fire, and old cooking fat!

Luckily for colonial women, soap was made only once or twice a year.

Colonial women rarely took baths!

Trying to take a bath was hard. A colonist would have to drag a tub to the fireside and then get enough water from the well to fill it. The water needed to be warmed, too. Instead, colonial women usually cleaned themselves with a cloth and bucket.

Colonial women made their own clothes.

Colonial women spun, dyed, and sewed wool and **flax** together to provide clothing for the whole family. A young girl would start learning how to spin at the age of 5.

Spinning Wheel

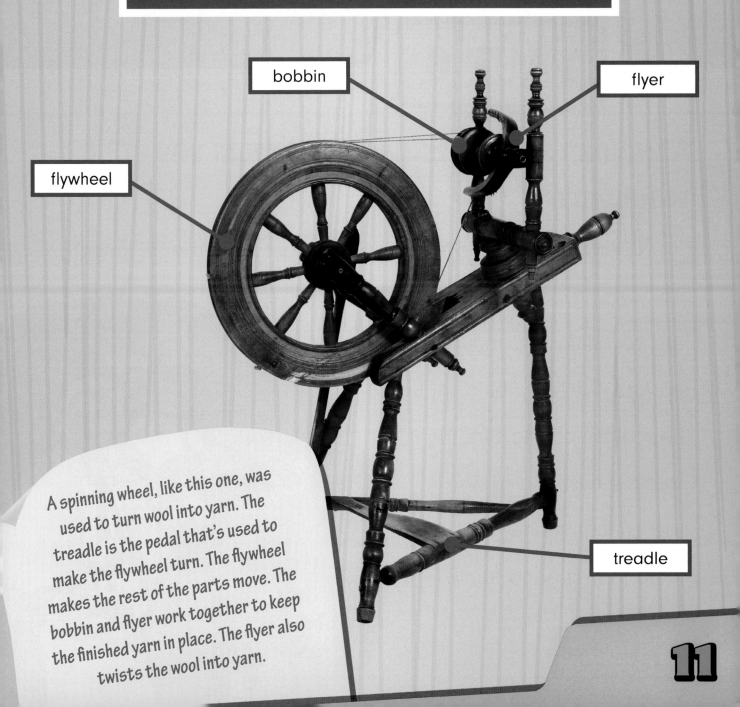

bobbin

flyer

flywheel

treadle

A spinning wheel, like this one, was used to turn wool into yarn. The treadle is the pedal that's used to make the flywheel turn. The flywheel makes the rest of the parts move. The bobbin and flyer work together to keep the finished yarn in place. The flyer also twists the wool into yarn.

Courtship

FACT 6

A woman's parents decided whom she would marry.

In colonial times, love wasn't important in marriage. In fact, many young people, men and women alike, had very little say about whom they married. Parents would set up the match, making sure the possible husband or wife had enough money and came from a good family.

Many women were married in a very simple ceremony called handfasting.

Lots of couples in colonial America didn't have the time or the money to plan a wedding. Instead of going to a church, a couple could simply hold hands and say together that they were married. Sometimes, handfasting occurred before a wedding, similar to an engagement.

George Washington married Martha Dandridge Custis in 1759 at a church in Virginia.

Adulthood and Motherhood

FACT 8

Girls as young as 13 were considered adults!

Girls were considered women and sometimes married by the time they were 13 or 14. Some women had to wait for older brothers and sisters to marry first, though. They might not marry until they were 20 or older.

The average woman gave birth to about seven children.

When the first settlers arrived in Virginia, there weren't any women with them! This quickly changed because, in order to create a successful colony, families were needed. When women did arrive in America, they began making big families.

In the colonies, many children died when they were still young.

FACT 10

In New England, girls were often taught reading but not writing.

New England colonists believed it was very important that women study the Bible, so they needed to know how to read.

In addition, girls learned important skills at home that helped them survive colonial life.

The schools girls attended in New England were called dame schools.

Quaker boys and girls went to different schools.

Quakers believed that girls and boys should both have

good schooling. However, that didn't mean that girls and boys

learned the same things! Girls went to schools that taught

important domestic skills.

Native American Women

Some Native American tribes were matrilineal.

In many Native American tribes, women were seen as more equal to men than in the colonies. In tribes such as the Iroquois, a person traced their family through their mother's side. When a man married, he went to live with his wife's family.

Native American women built houses.

Women of many different Native American tribes worked hard gathering what was needed to build and care for a home. They also made tools, blankets, baskets, and pots—all while caring for their family!

Pocahontas is one of the best-known Native American women from the colonial period. Captain John Smith wrote that she saved his life, but historians believe it was unlikely she was even there at the time!

Black Women in Colonial America

FACT 14

Some of the first African women in colonial America weren't brought as slaves.

The Dutch brought African women to their colony of New Amsterdam in the 1620s. The women weren't there to work, but to keep the male slaves company! Other black women were brought to Virginia and other colonies as **indentured servants**.

Phillis Wheatley was the first slave to publish poetry in colonial America.

Phillis Wheatley was brought to Boston, Massachusetts, from western Africa when she was about 7. She was sold to the Wheatley family, who educated her. In 1773, she published the book *Poems on Various Subjects.*

Phillis Wheatley was freed in 1773.

Businesswomen

FACT 16

Some women in colonial America were entrepreneurs!

Unmarried women and widows had more rights than married women in colonial America. They could own property, write wills, and run their own businesses! Women worked as **seamstresses** and even owned shops.

Mary Alexander was a shop owner. She helped her first husband in his business until he died and continued to sell goods after she married her second husband.

In many towns, women controlled the press!

There are many accounts of women who were accomplished printers of newspapers and books. Clementina Rind, who printed the *Virginia Gazette*, also published Thomas Jefferson's *A Summary View of the Rights of British America in 1774.*

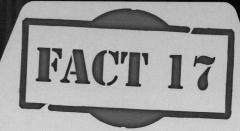

Women in the Revolution

FACT 18

Women were spies during the American Revolution!

Because women weren't considered as smart as men, men often talked about secret military plans in front of them, believing the women didn't understand. This made women perfect for spying! **Loyalist** Ann Bates is still remembered for the secrets she uncovered.

"Molly Pitcher" was likely a nickname for the many women who helped soldiers in the American Revolution.

While "Molly Pitcher" wasn't just one person, some of the stories about her may come from the life of Mary McCauley. She followed her husband from battle to battle, and when he was wounded, she manned a gun in his place.

Margaret Corbin was another brave colonial woman. Her husband was killed in an American Revolution battle, and she took his place at a cannon!

FACT 20

One hero of the American Revolution was 16-year-old Sybil Ludington.

Sybil's father was the head of the local **militia**. On the night of April 26, 1777, he learned the British were attacking the town of Danbury, Connecticut. Sybil rode 40 miles (64 km) in the pouring rain to gather troops. By morning, about 400 men had arrived to fight off the British.

Sybil Ludington rode farther than Paul Revere did on his historic ride!

Legendary Colonial Women

Mary Alexander
successful shop owner

Margaret Corbin
took husband's place in battle

Phillis Wheatley
first published slave poet

Clementina Rind
successful printer

Sybil Ludington
rode to gather militia to fight the British

Ann Bates
British spy

Many of these colonial women's names aren't commonly known, but they had an effect on history!

Creating a Life in a New World

Colonial women couldn't vote, weren't given much education, and were considered less than men. Their parts in history are often overlooked in history books, though their lives were just as challenging as men's—perhaps even more so!

Colonial women *did* have an impact on history. They ran households, worked in the fields, built houses, published newspapers, and raised the future citizens of the United States. Their strength and bravery were an important part of the founding of our country.

Today in Colonial Williamsburg in Virginia, women dress in colonial clothing to show visitors what life was like in colonial America.

29

Glossary

colonial: having to do with colonies, which were lands under the control of another country

domestic: of the home, dealing with skills, chores, or pursuits that have to do with the house

entrepreneur: a person who runs his or her own business

flax: a piece of the flax plant that can be cleaned and used to make thread and cloth

indentured servant: a person who pays for their passage across the ocean by working for someone else for several years without pay

ingredient: a food that is mixed with other foods

Loyalist: someone who was on the side of the British during the American Revolution

matrilineal: tracing descent through the mother's side

militia: a volunteer group of soldiers

seamstress: a women who sews clothes and other items as a job

trencher: a wooden dish that colonial people used as a plate or bowl

For More Information

Books

Raum, Elizabeth. *The Dreadful, Smelly Colonies: The Disgusting Details About Life During Colonial America.* Mankato: MN: Capstone Press, 2010.

Roberts, Cokie. *Founding Mothers: Remembering the Ladies.* New York, NY: Harper, 2014.

Websites

Colonial Williamsburg: Family
www.history.org/Almanack/life/family/background.cfm
Learn about the different families in colonial America, and find out more about the roles of women in America.

Colonial Women
www.landofthebrave.info/colonial-women.htm
Learn more about the daily life of colonial women, and find out the differences between living life as a Puritan, a wealthy woman, and more!

National Women's History Museum: Colonial Period
www.nwhm.org/education-resources/biography/colonial-period
Learn the life stories of some of the most exciting women of the colonial era!

Index